In Loving Memory of
Edward P. Rousseau Jr.

It was a very cold
and snowy day. I
woke up early as
usual. Our house
was quiet and my
sisters were still
asleep. Dad was
asleep too. My
Mom... well that's
another story.

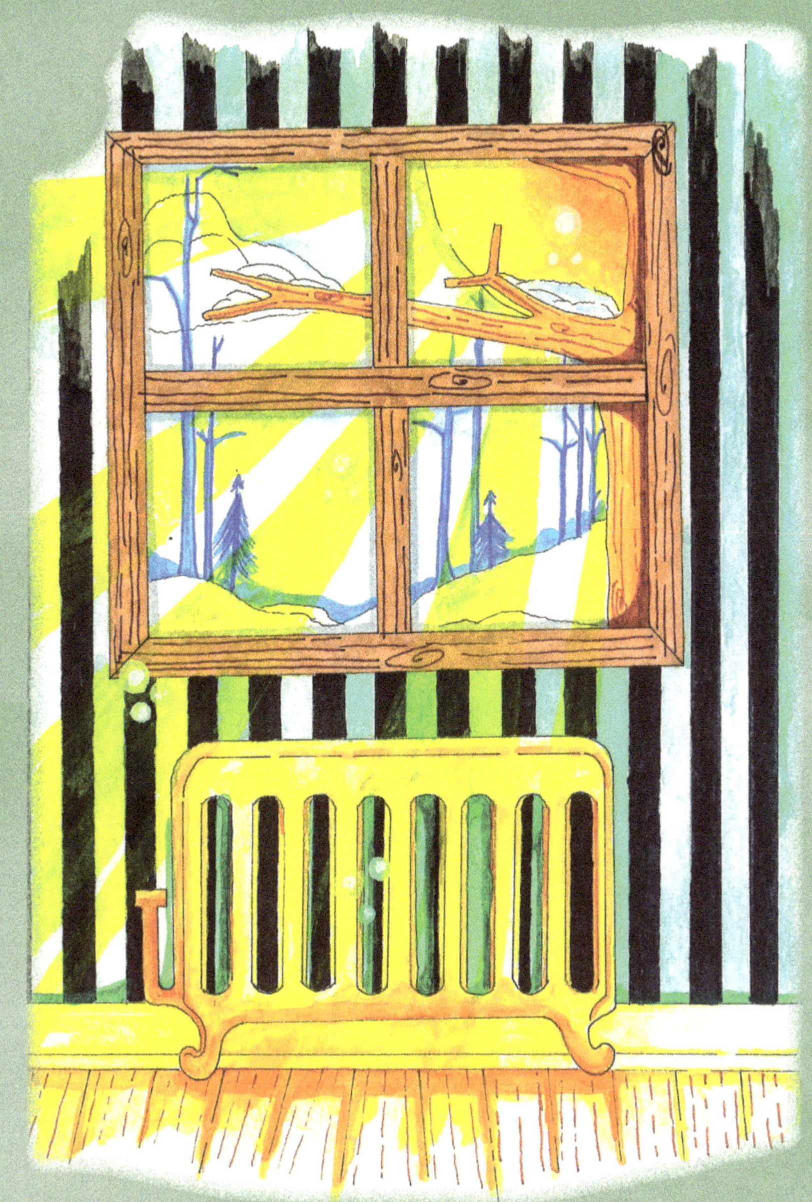

It is the weekend and Dad slept in a little later. When Dad woke up, my sisters and I help him with the chores around the house. My sisters clean and I sweep

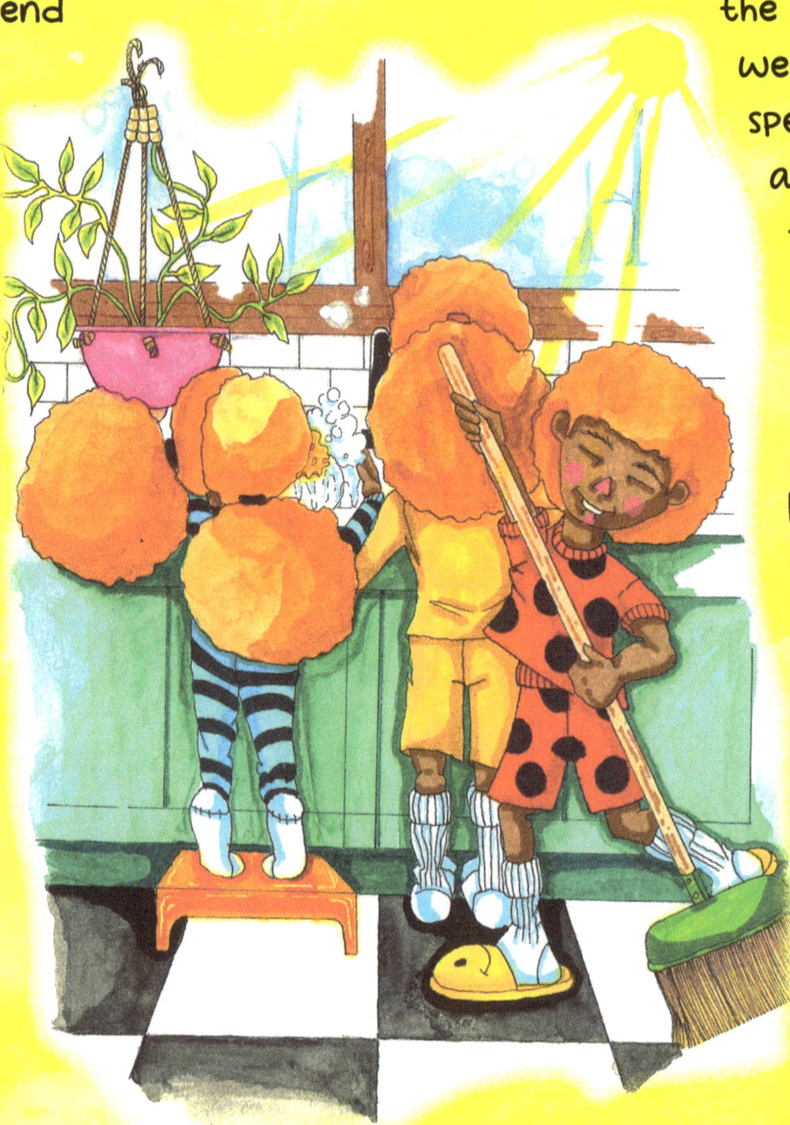

the kitchen. This weekend was special. We all wanted the house to be clean for what Dad calls Anniversary. He said it comes every year and it's our "happy/sad" day.

When I finished
sweeping, I asked
to go outside. My
sisters came with
me after they
finished cleaning.
Whenever we
went outside,
Dad always said
the same thing.
"Be careful and
stay near the
house," he would
say in his deep
voice.

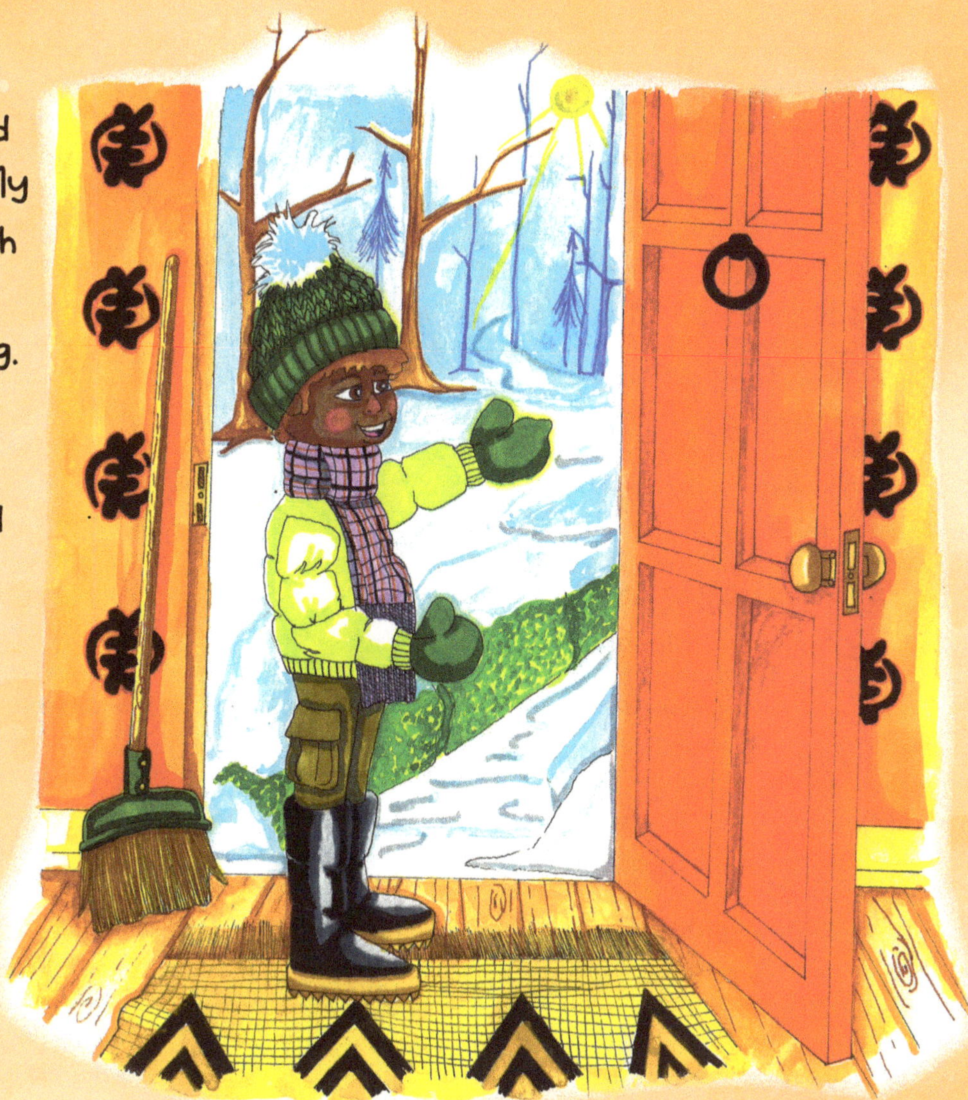

"Make sure you look after Trevor, girls," Dad said. "We don't want any experiences like we've had before, do we Trevor?" That's me Trevor. Sometimes, when we go outside, I feel like I am in my own little world and forget about what Dad tells me. In the past, I may have even wandered off a few times so my sisters' would get upset and yell, "Pay attention!"

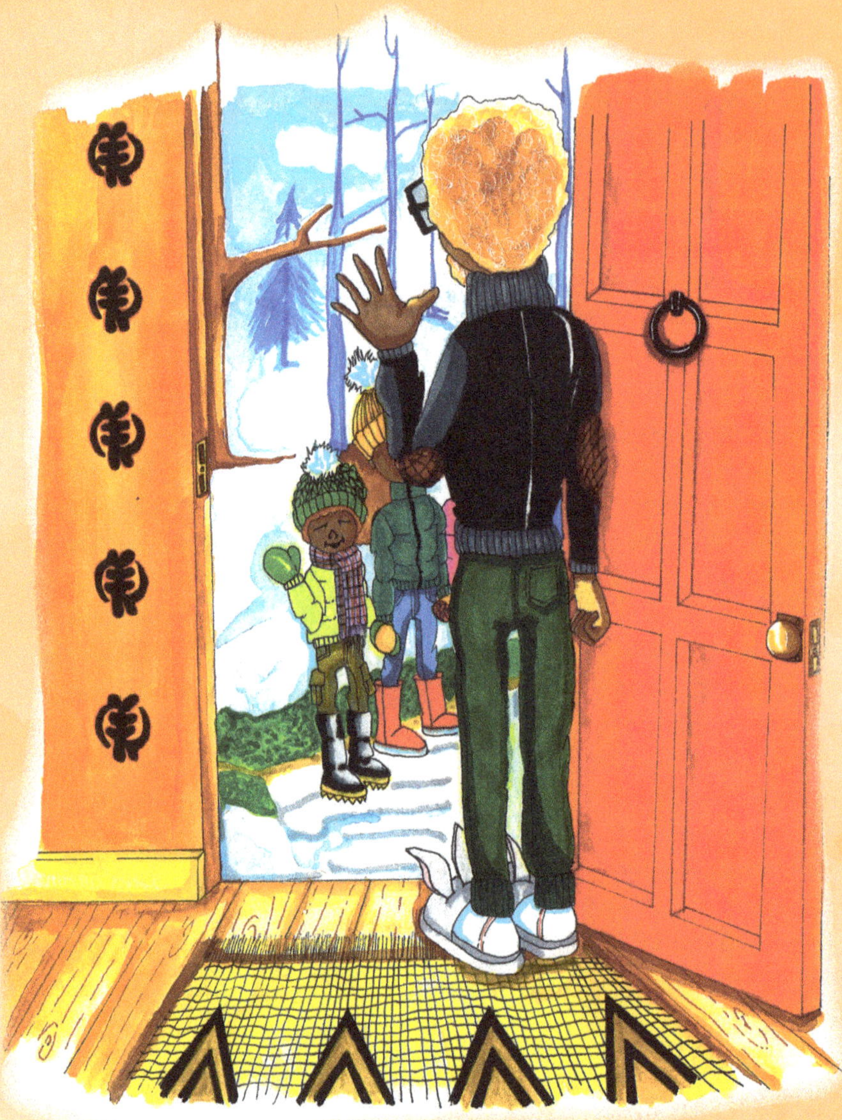

4

I think that's why people
in my neighborhood
would say that I
was "different"
or "special." I
never heard
my sisters call
me funny
names, but the
neighborhood
children would
call me that
or worse. The
name calling
made me feel
bad at first,
but my sisters
took up for me
every time.

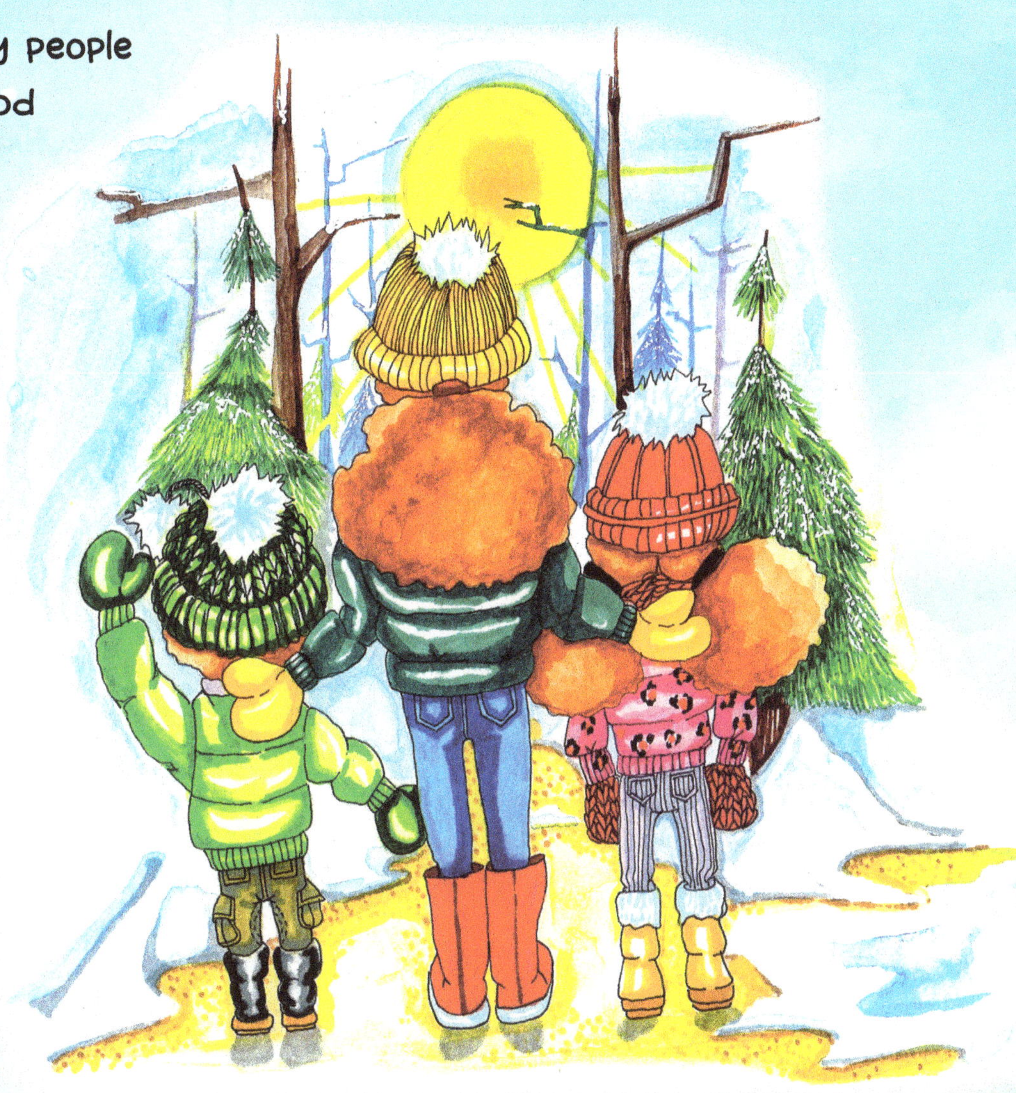

When we get to the park, the snow is about two feet high. It looked like it had been snowing for two days straight. Stephanie, one of my sisters, always holds my hand when we walked, so I wouldn't run off. She said with sass, "Don't make me have to come and find you" and I would do my best to get away. Sheila, my older sister, is the boss of us at the park and Stephanie is the boss of me. The park was packed. We were having a ball. Children were playing tag, building snowmen, making snow angels, and throwing snowballs. I want to join, but I felt nervous.

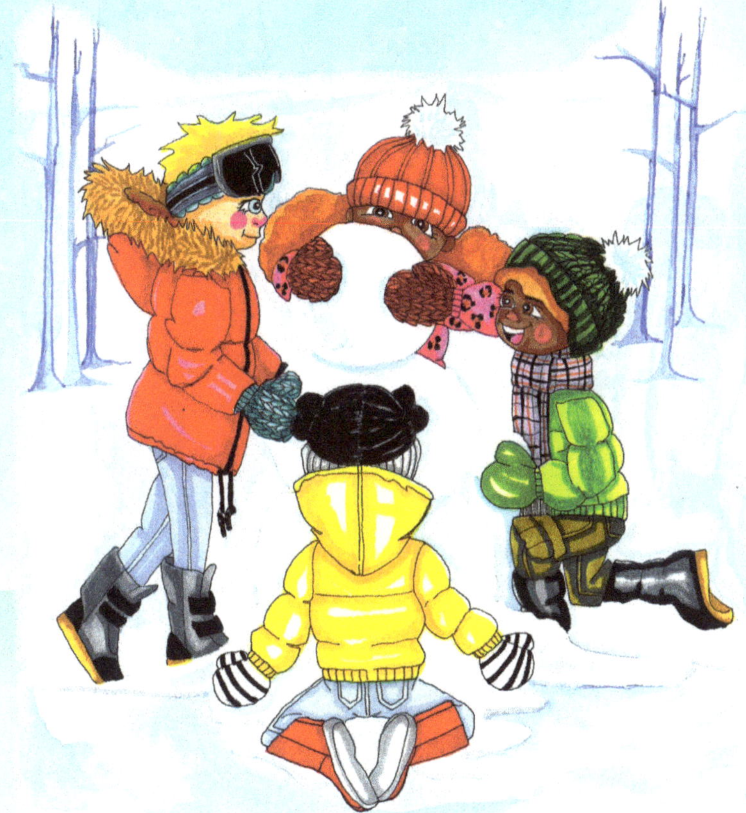

Sheila pushes me toward a group making a snowman. I pushed away, but she shoved me as close as possible. We start to help the children making the snowman. Stephanie works on the top and I work on the bottom with some other children. When we finish the snowman, Stephanie yelled out to all of us, "Our snowman should be a girl."

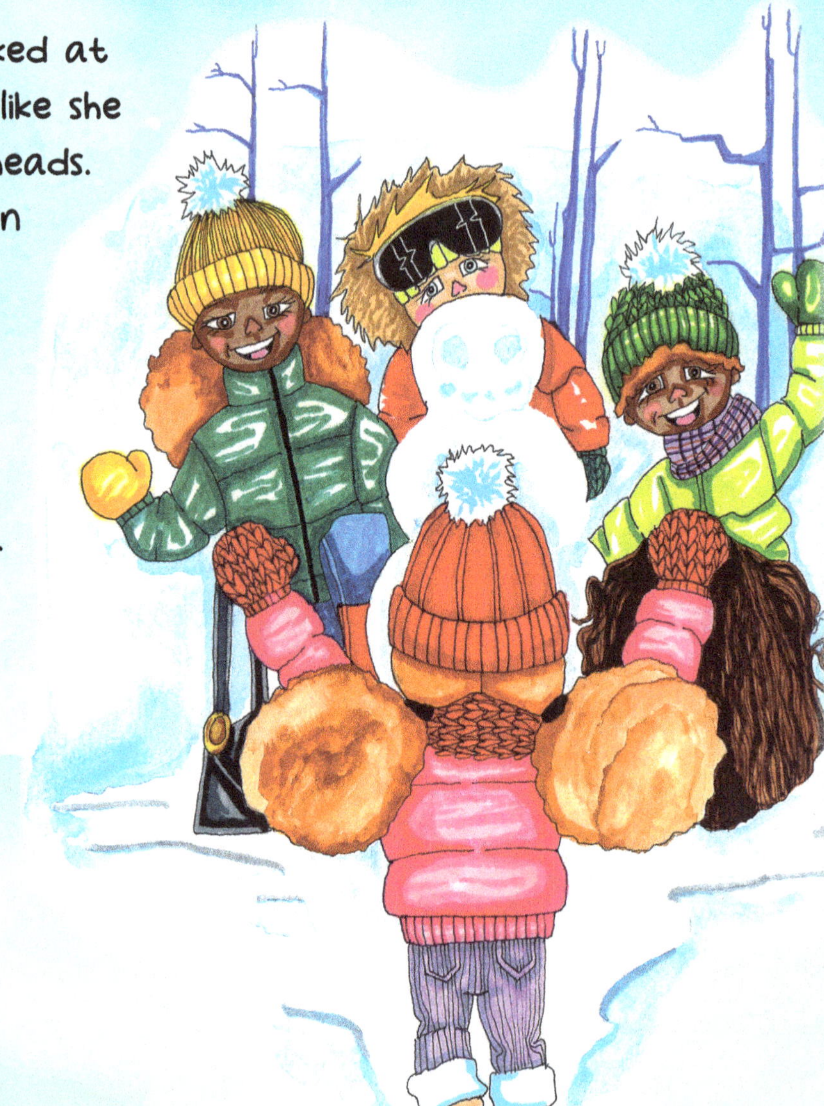

We all looked at Stephanie like she had two heads. The children began to argue. Stephanie said,"Let's take a vote!" Our neighbor Billy said," Stephanie there is no such thing as a girl snowman."

Stephanie didn't listen one bit. She made all the girls vote and they won. "Girls rule. Girls rule", a bunch of girls shouted. Stephanie ran to the house and asked my dad for one an of my Moms's old pocketbooks and her old wig.

Then she ran to a garbage can in the park and pulled out a purple, dusty hat with a feather. She placed the wig and the hat on the snowman's head and wrapped her scarf around its neck. Next, she put the pocketbook on the side of the snowman. She found a broken pair of glasses on the ground and put them on the snowman's face.

"Well now we have a snow woman". Stephanie said. Thats when sheila came over and told us it was time to go. She looked at the snow woman and said." Wow I've never seen a SNOW MA'AM. All the children laughed.

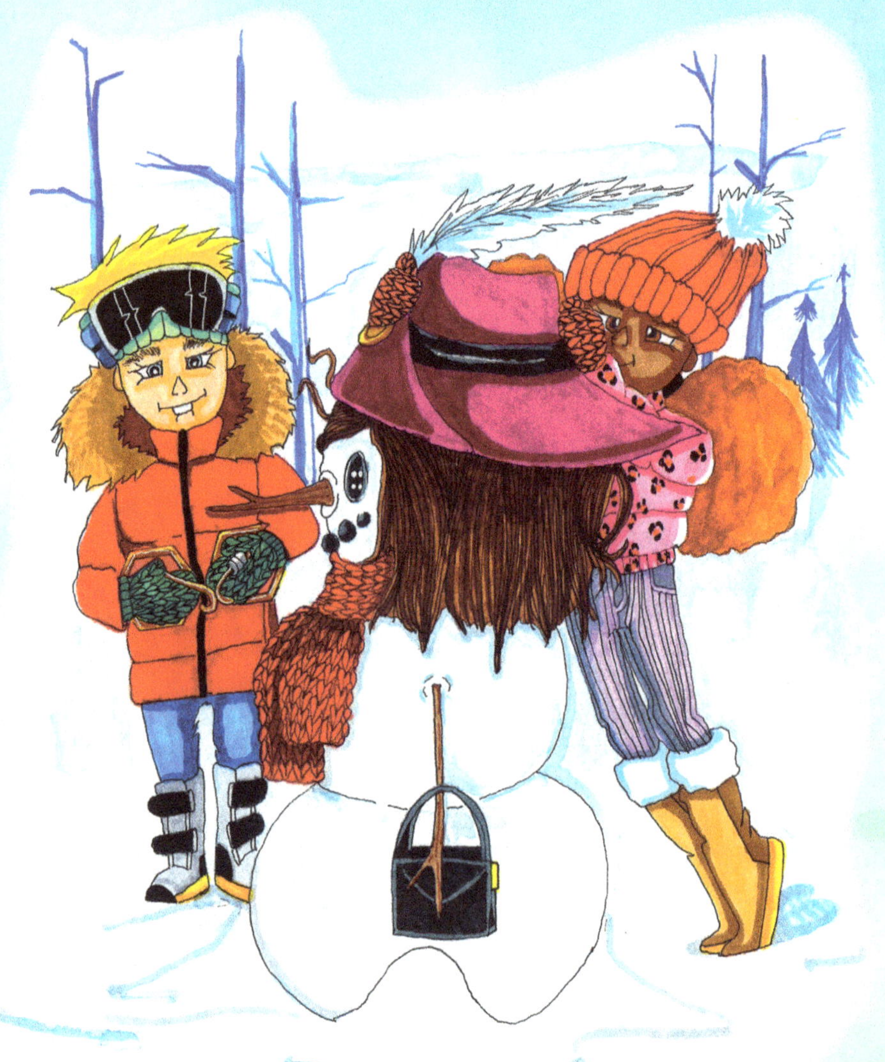

10

As we left the park,
Stephanie waived
goodbye to our new
SnowMa'am and we
made our way home.

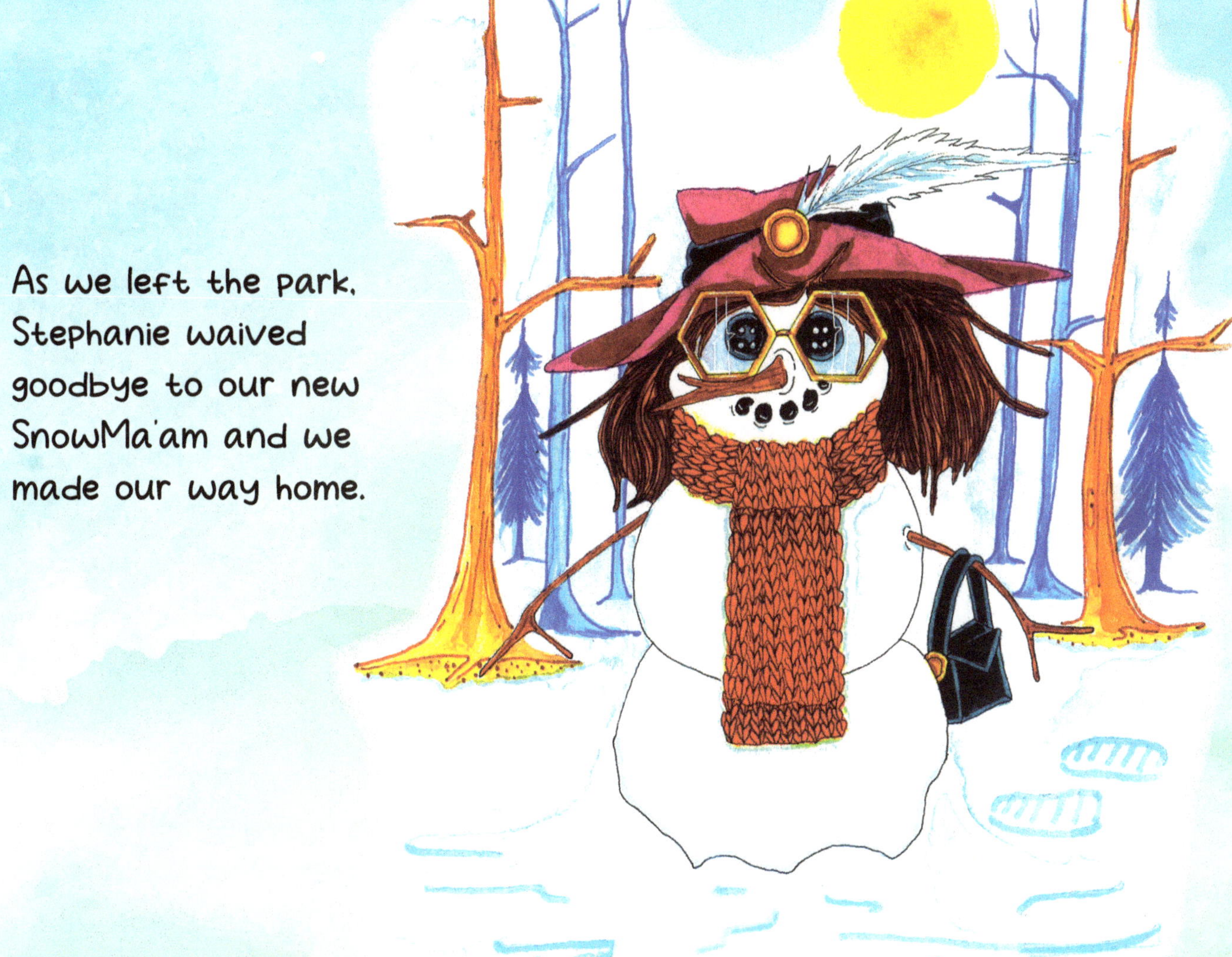

11

After dinner, we told Dad about "SnowMa'aM". He laughed as he listened to our story. "That was one of the funniest stories I heard in a long time. I needed that laugh Steph", he said. He turned to her and said, "I loved that you thought on your own terms. Good job." That's when Sheila opened her mouth and said, "Dad, then why would we ever call this a sad day?" Dad told Sheila that all of us being together, always made it a beautiful day. Stephanie added ,"Uh, what about Mom?" Dad didn't answer and had a funny look on his face, like he didn't want to hear what Stephanie had just said. We all ignored her and kept busy. After cleaning and showering. Dad told us,"Love you all, time for bed."

That night I could not fall asleep.
Stephanie and Sheila kept talking
about Mom. Every year on this
day, Stephanie and Sheila
talked about things
our Mom had told
them. Their voices
would fill the
hallway. Soon
after my Dad
would come to
our rooms and
tell us to go to
sleep. My sisters
would fake like
they were sleep
until he left the
room. Soon as
the door closed,
I would hear
them pop back
up and start
chatting again.

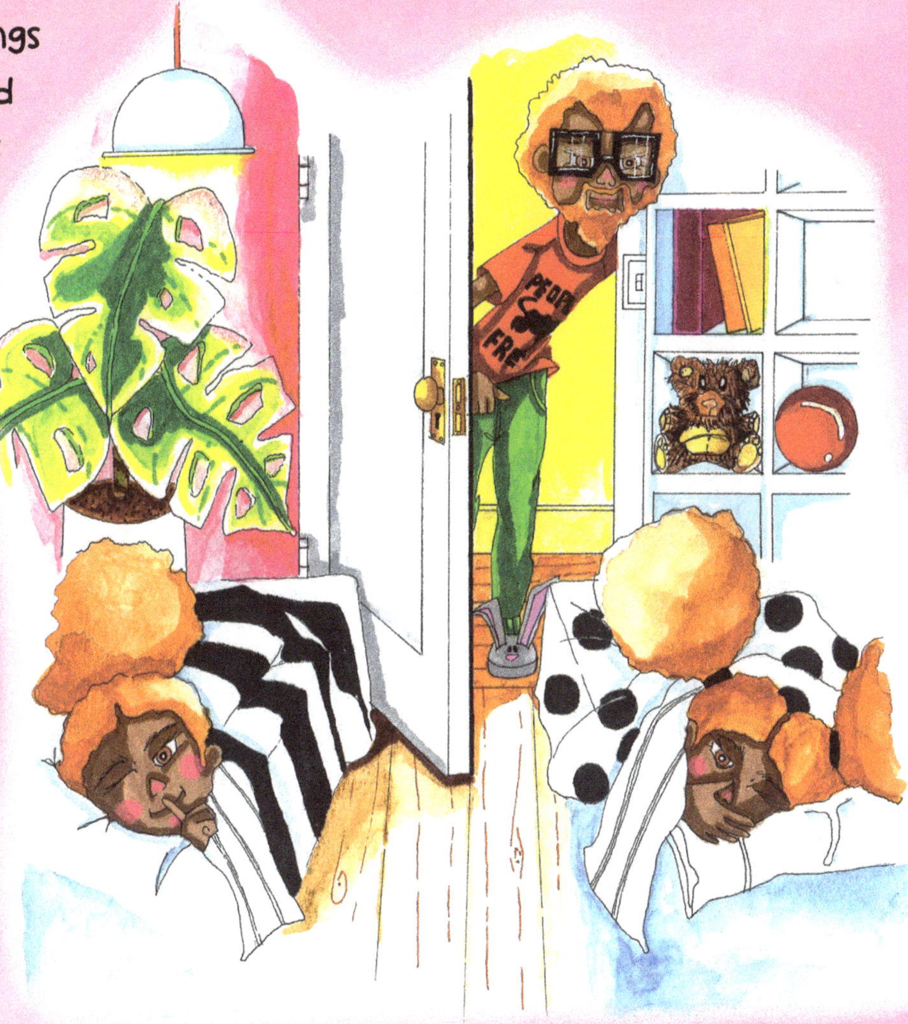

When I drifted off to sleep, I started to dream. It felt like it was real. Suddenly, I was in the park again, but this time it was just me. No Stephanie. No Sheila. I thought I was alone in the park, but I couldn't help but feel, a pair of eyes looking at me. When I turned around I saw a big, white face, with big black eyes and a wide smile staring back at me. The face began to laugh and held its belly that shook. It looked like the snowman... snow woman we made earlier. It scared me half to death. Just as I started to run, it let out a noise. I could tell the noises were words. It said," Don't be scared chile',I don't bite. My mouth fell open and I rubbed my eyes.

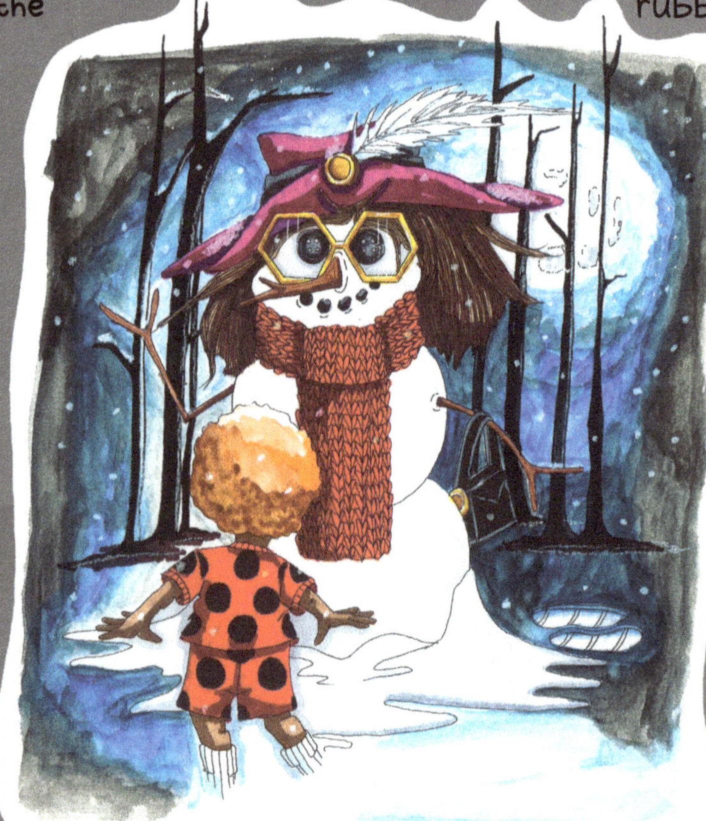

My heart beat like a drum. I felt like running but my feet would not move. It looked and sounded like an old woman. She looked down, grabbed me and hugged me."I've been waiting for a friend to talk to." she said. My eyes opened widely. " My name is Bessie." The snow woman said. "Besillia Mae Duncan. Bessie for short. What's your name son?"

14

"T-t-t-t... Trevor Mam, I mean, Miss SnowMa'aM." She belted a hearty laugh and reached down to grab my hand. Out of nowhere, SnowMa'am and I were back at my house. We stood in the living room. It was lit by the tree that had a star at the top. It looked like an actual star in the sky. The tree smelled really good and presents were underneath it.

SnowMa'aM looked at me and said "I miss the smells and these colors dearly!" She moved slowly towards me as she began to speak." Trevor, I have been waiting for someone to call on me. Your gift has brought me back". I thought to myself, I guess that's why they call me special. She smiled widely with teeth all made with rocks. She noticed the record player towards the corner of the living room. Dad had a few records sitting on the side of the turntable. She picked up a jazz record, placed it on the platter, and gently lowered the needle.

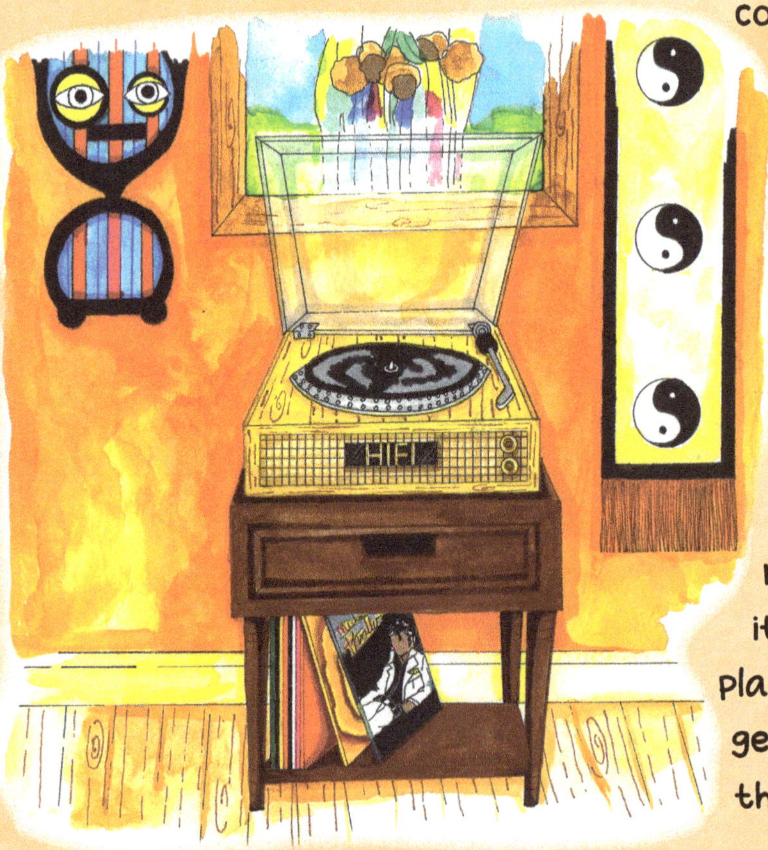

She scooped me up when the music started to play. We danced to what she said was her favorite song. I didn't believe her, because it was the oldest record we had. It cracked and skipped. A man named Dizzy was blowing a horn and singing about peanuts or something. We danced around in my living room to his symphony. I shivered as I looked up at SnowMa'aM. At that moment, thought I recognized her voice. "Duncan", I said, "... Is my last name." The wide smile I saw on SnowMa'am's face warmed my soul. Not only did I recognize her voice, but I recognized her smile.

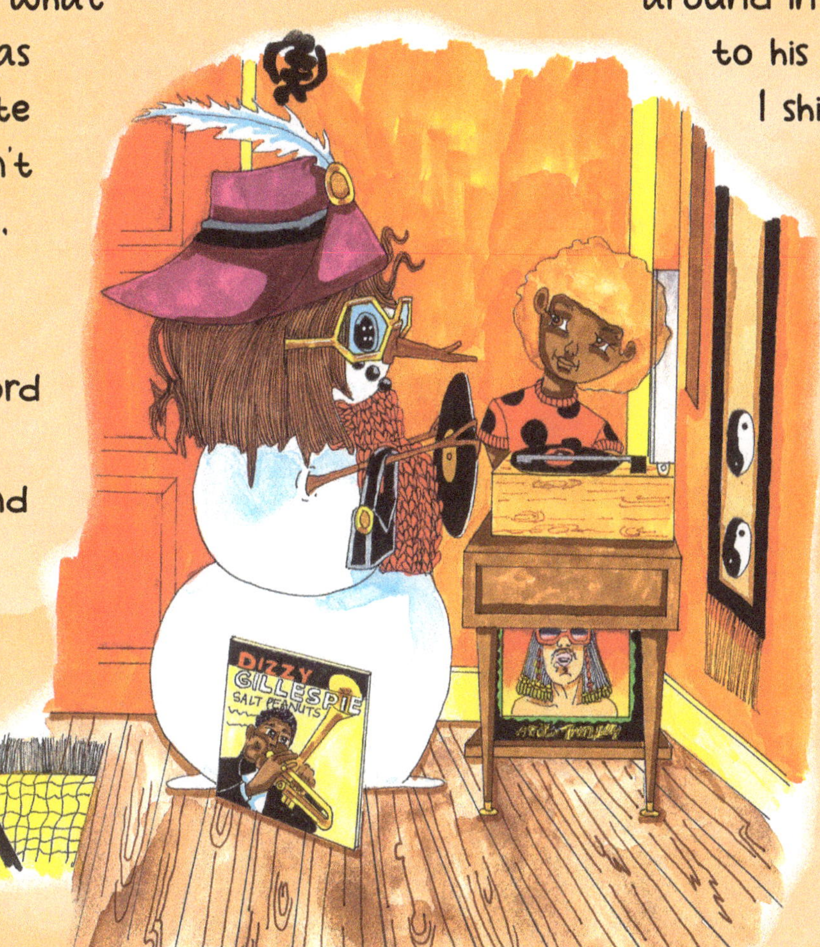

I grinned wide
enough to put
the star on
the top of
the tree
to shame. I
jumped into
her arms and
squeezed
her fluffy
white coat
of snow
until my
arms were
full. "She's
back, she's
back!" I
screamed,
but
SnowMa'aM

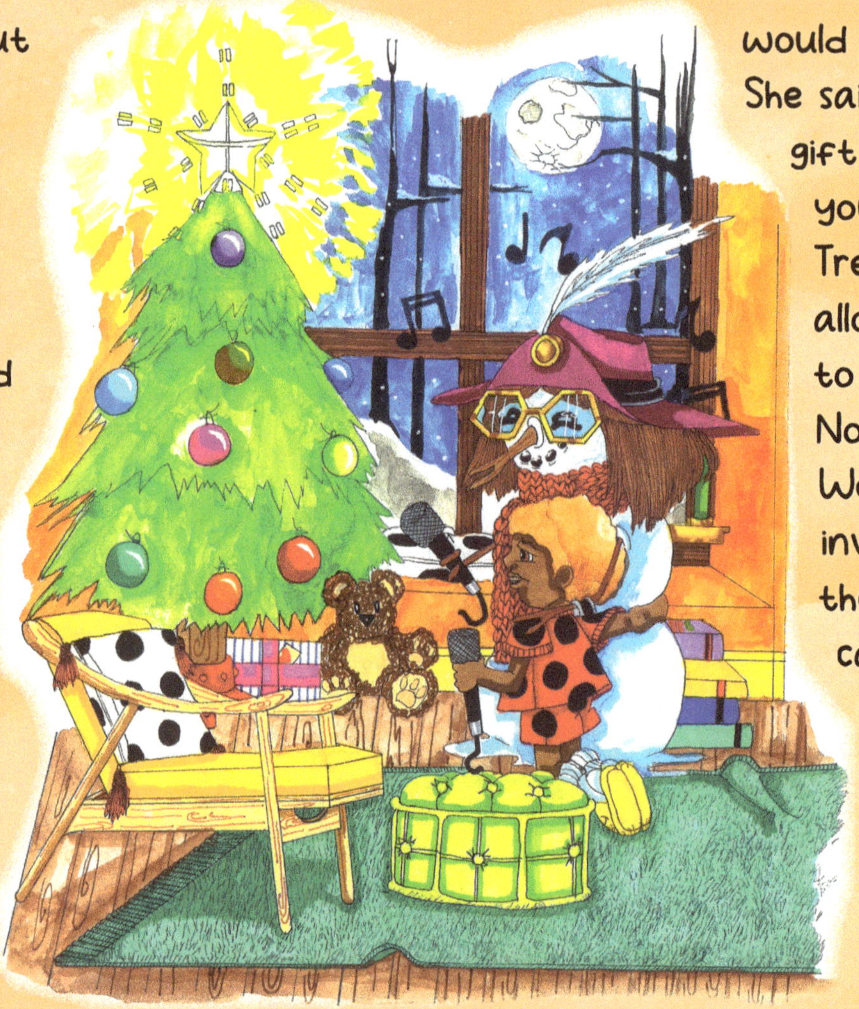

told me, no one
would hear me.
She said, "The
gift that
you have
Trevor, only
allows you
to see me.
No one else.
We are
invisible to
them. We
can see
them
but
they
can't
see us."

"Mommy", I squeaked. "Yes Trevor, you were very young when I left", she said. That's when she cuddled me like I was her newborn baby. "This is so wonderful that I can see you all once again. Ed, Sheila, Stephanie and my baby", she said. "All I did while I was gone, was wish to see you all again. You made it happen Trevor," as she hugged me with all her snowiness.

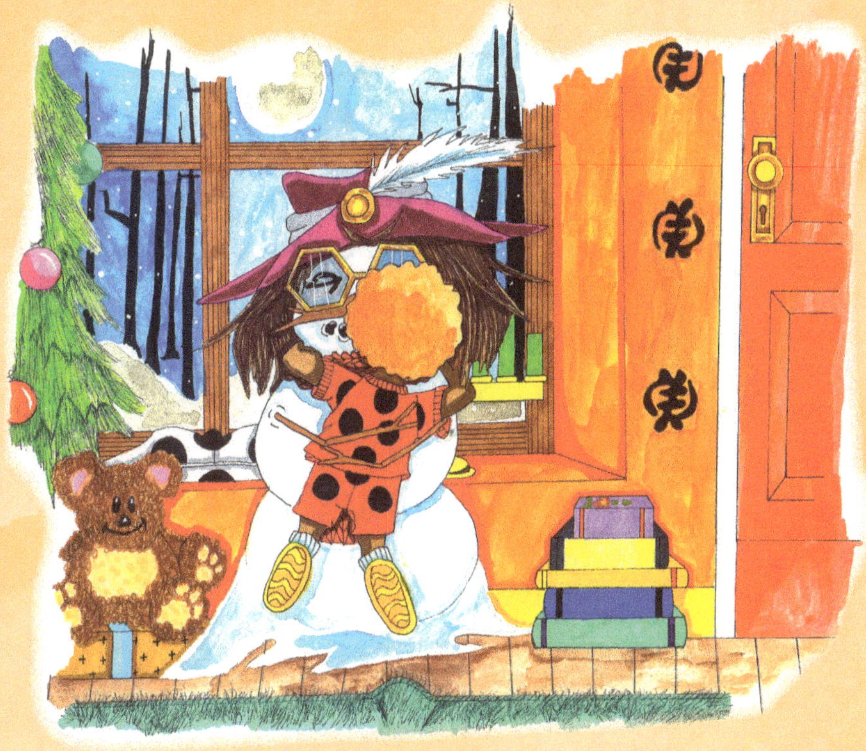

It felt strange watching everyone asleep, while we were having such a great time. We danced, sang songs, and she even told me a story about how she and my dad met. We were having so much fun, we didn't realize it would be morning soon. I began to think to myself, Is SnowMa'aM gonna leave? I started to miss her

already. We took a long last look at the family sleeping. SnowMa'am whispered, " I love them so."
We quietly scooted out the girls room.

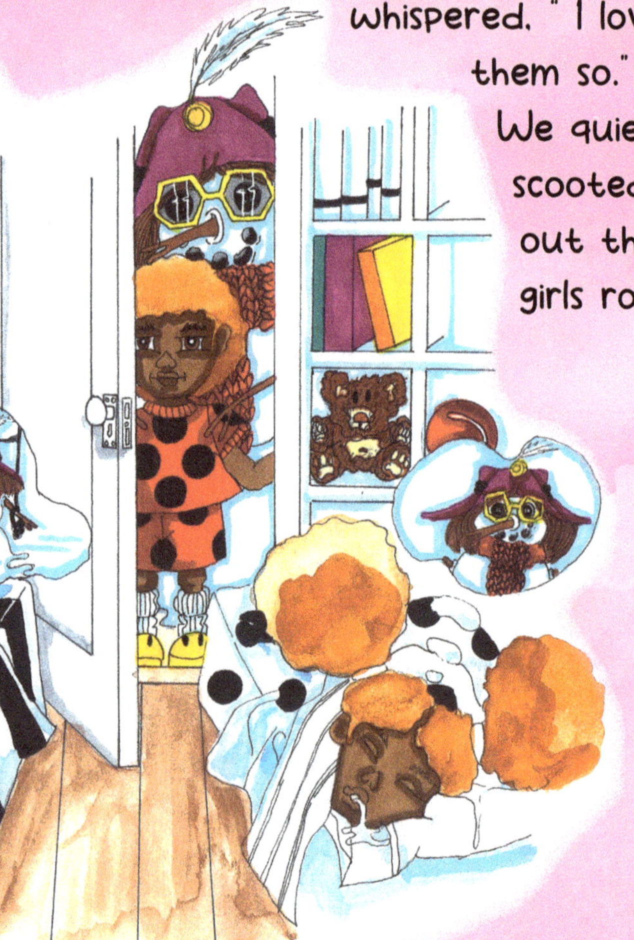

SnowMa'am
bent down and
picked me up.
She brought
me close to her
powdery face.
Her buttoned
eyes looked
right into mine
and she said,"
Trevor I will
always love
you and your
sisters'. I am so
proud of you
Trevor. Seeing
you has made
me the happiest
snow woman
on earth. When
you wake
Trevor I will not
be here.

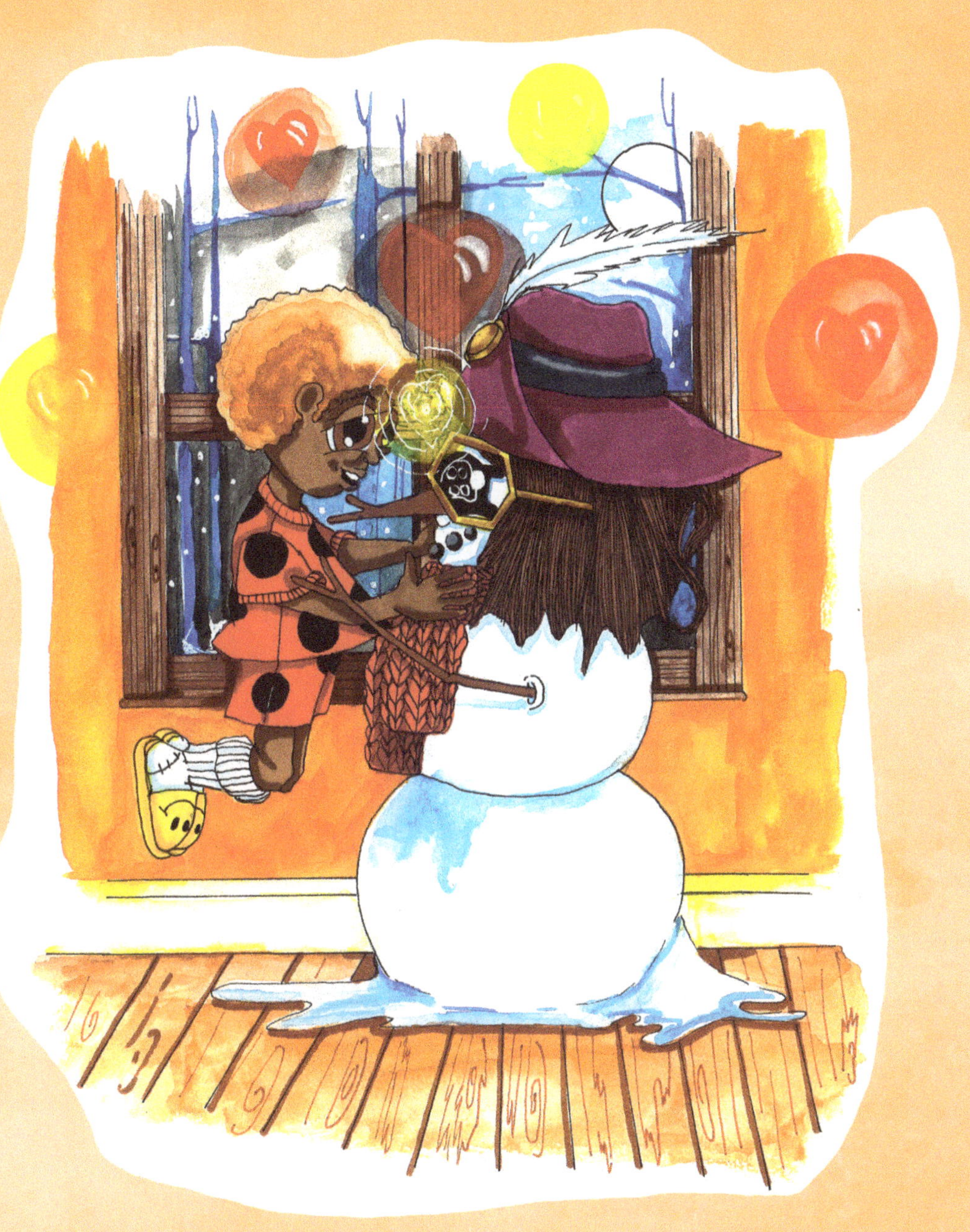

"I will miss you with all my iced heart." SnowMa'am held back her icy tears as she put me down. I gasped and held back my tears. She took my hand and slowly moved toward the door. Then she turned to look back at her old home. She looked at me and said, "You keep this family sound and loving Trevor, that is your job."

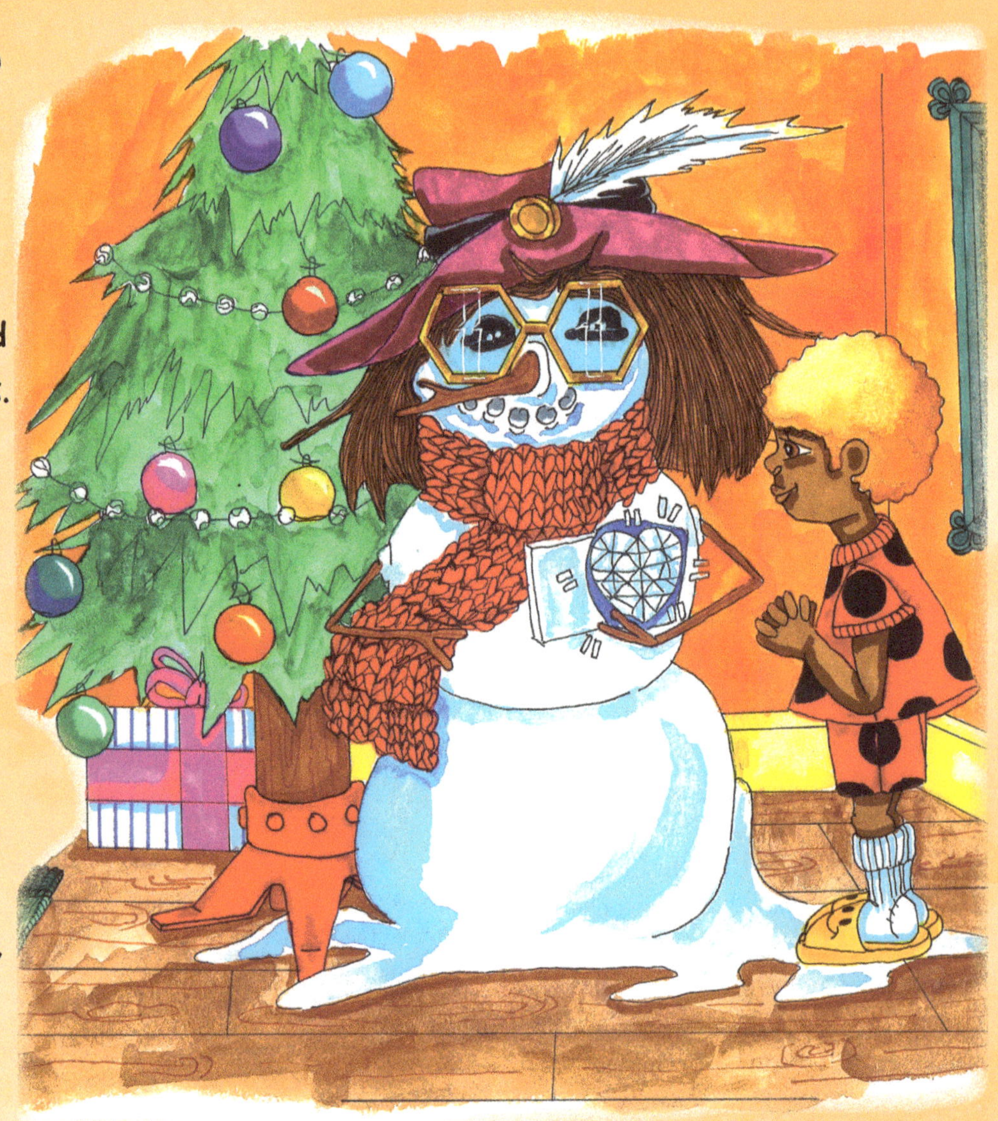

I answered with a quiet," Yes Ma'am". As SnowMa'aM moved closer to the door, a light was beaming brightly through the crack at the bottom. She said, "Trevor, it's time." I held her snowy hand as long as I could. SnowMa'aM opened the door and in a Zap, she was gone. It was like a vacuum sucked her straight into the air. Poof. At the same time, I wound up back in my bed. It was 6 o'clock in the morning and I could hear movement in the hall.

I jumped up and ran to where the noise was coming from, praying it was SnowMa'aM, but it wasn't. Sheila was up early heading to the bathroom. She spotted me and said, "What are you doing up?" I ran over to her and jumped into her arms and gave her a gigantic hug. " What is wrong with you?" she said sounding puzzled. I told her I had the best dream I could ever have.

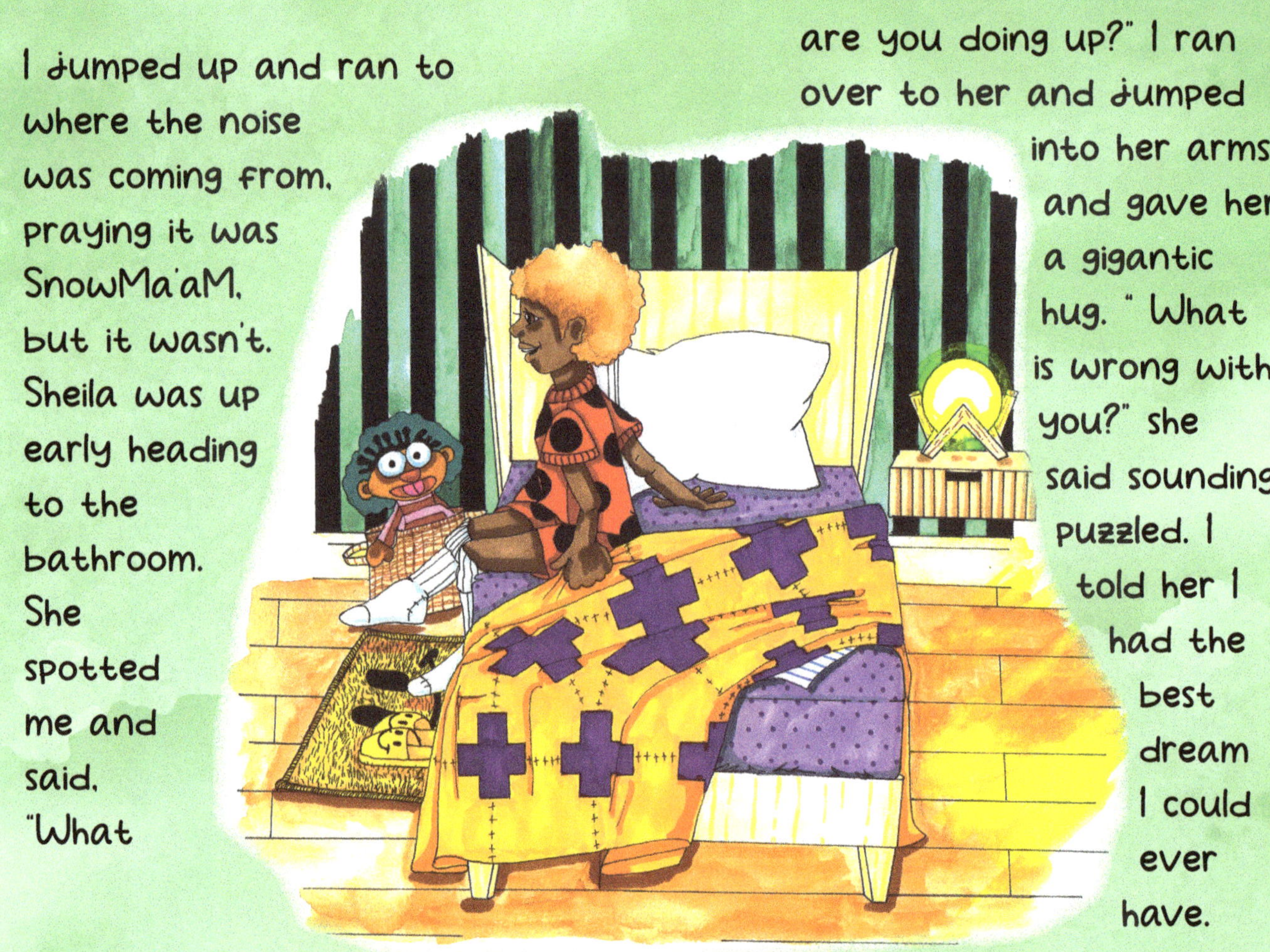

That's when Dad came out of his room. He said. "What's all the ruckus about this morning?You guys seem to be eager this morning to get the chores done. As he put his glasses on. I began telling him what had happened in my dream last night. The girls thought it was a cute dream. Stephanie laughed. Sheila made fun of me and Dad smiled. but looked at me curiously. I continued to explain to him how real the dream felt. It felt as real as speaking with him and my sisters.

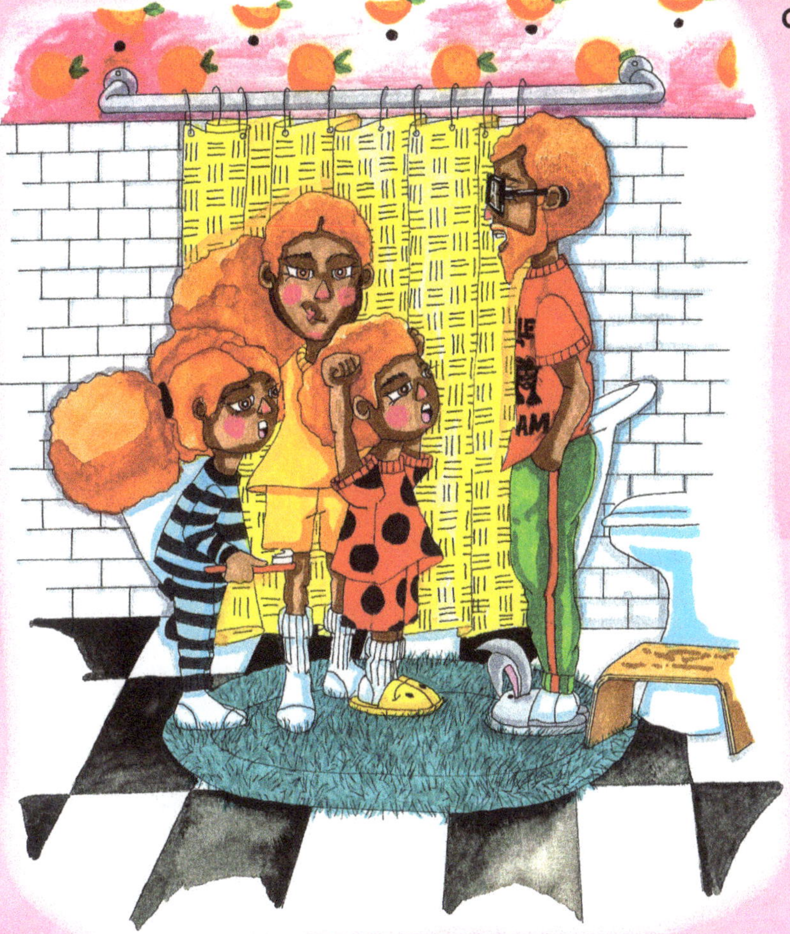

Then we all looked out
the window. We saw
SnowMa'aM in the
park, frigid and alone
with her ice glistening.
Sheila pointed and
said,
"SnowMa'aM is going
nowhere til spring."
We all laughed as
Stephanie headed to
the kitchen to start
breakfast.

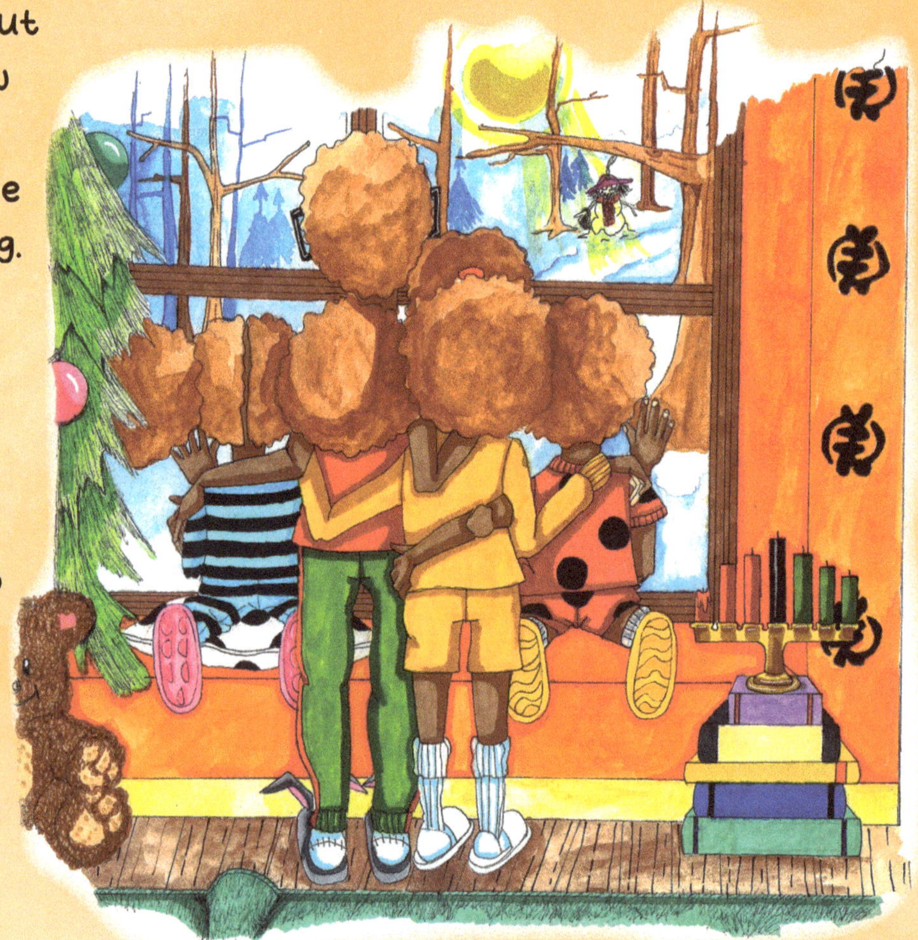

As she left
the living room
and passed the
turntable, it was
spinning and had
a record on it.
She stopped and
said, "That's odd,
who was listening
to records this
morning???"

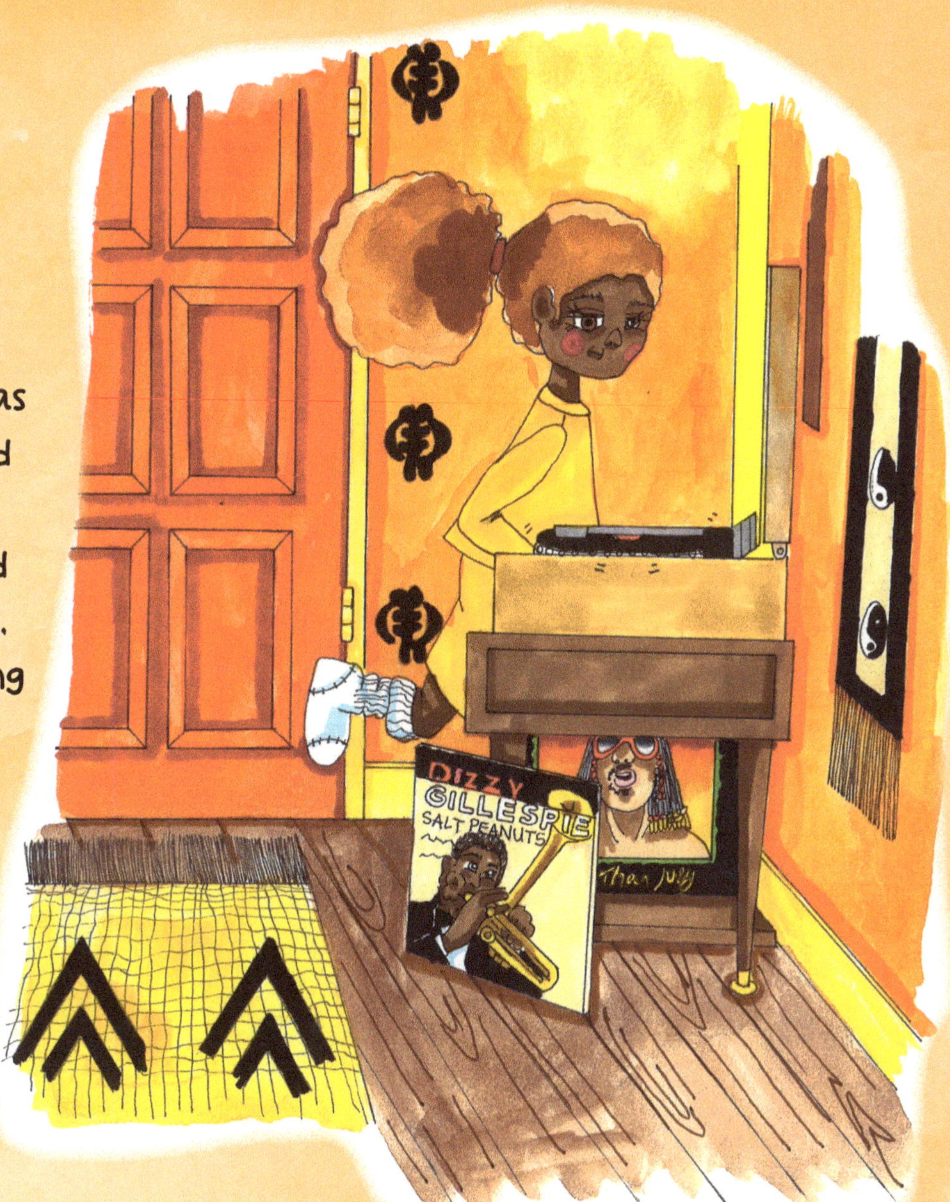

The End

Part 1

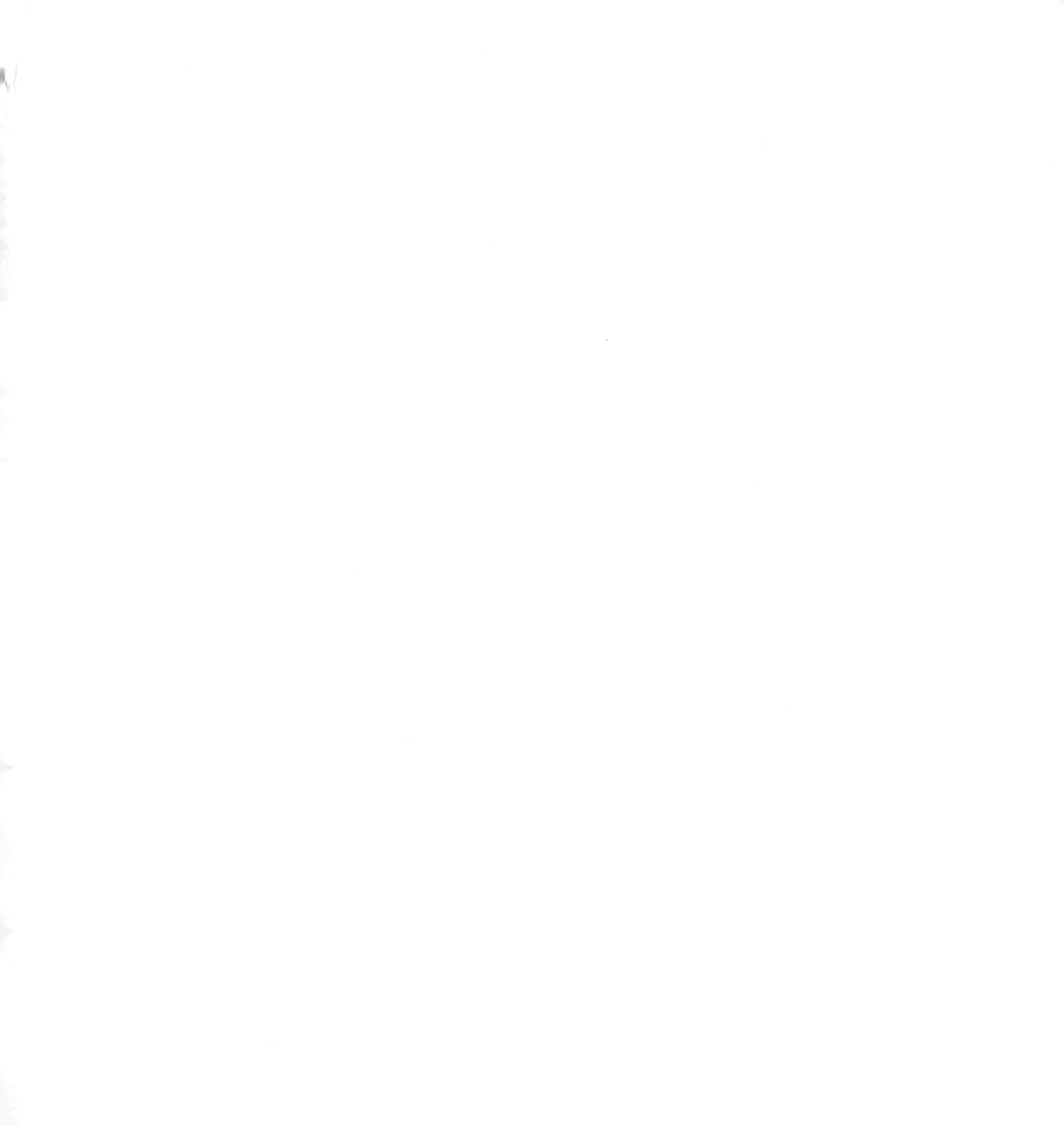